DEPRESSION IS THE PITS, BUT I'M GETTING BETTER

A Guide for Adolescents

◆ ◆ ◆

E. Jane Garland, M.D.

Magination Press ◆ Washington, DC

Acknowledgements

The author is grateful to all those young people who shared their experiences, their stories, their photos, and their drawings. Special thanks to Doris Ling and Frederick Fung of Bodwell College and to their teacher David G. Crawford. The encouragement of Dr. Margaret Weiss and my other colleagues in the Mood and Anxiety Disorders Clinic is greatly appreciated. The BC Children's Hospital Children's Miracle Telethon Fund supported the psychoeducational project out of which this book was conceived.

Library of Congress Cataloging-in-Publication Data
Garland, E. Jane.
    Depression is the pits, but I'm getting better : a guide for adolescents / E. Jane Garland.
        p.   cm.
    Includes bibliographical references.
    Summary: Discusses the difference between being sad and suffering from clinical depression, how to gain control over this condition, the use of medications and psychotherapy, and the experiences of depressed teens.
    ISBN 1-55798-458-1
    1. Depression in adolescence--Juvenile literature.
[1. Depression, Mental.]   I. Title.
RJ506.D4G37   1997
616.85'27'00835--dc21   96-40188
                                                         CIP
                                                         AC

Published by
MAGINATION PRESS
An Educational Publishing Foundation Book
American Psychological Association
750 First Street, NE
Washington, DC 20002

Manufactured in the United States of America
10 9 8 7 6 5 4 3 2 1

CONTENTS

◆

INTRODUCTION

◆

Maybe you've said, or heard someone else say, "I'm so depressed about that." That is not quite the same thing as what we call Depression, or Clinical Depression. This book will explain what the difference is, and how to tell if you might have clinical depression. It also explains more about what causes depression, and how to get rid of it.

If you are reading this, it is probably because someone has told you that you have clinical depression. Or perhaps you are reading this because you think you might have it. Maybe you are concerned about a friend who is depressed.

This book will answer many of your questions. But if you want to know more, ask your doctor, psychiatrist, psychologist, or other counselor.

Depression is serious. It is hard on your physical health, and it makes everything you do so much harder to get through. That is why we want to recognize it and start treatment as quickly as possible.

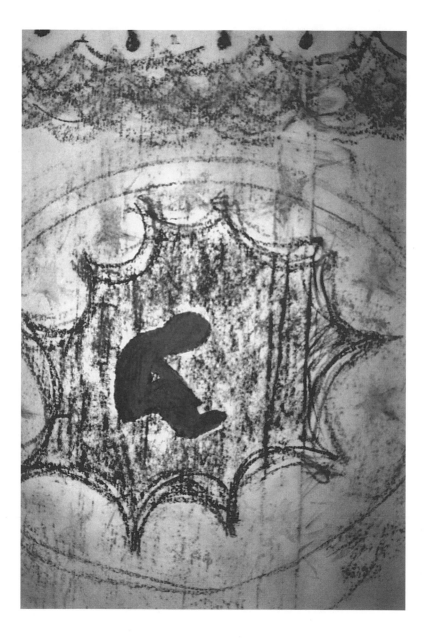

1.

UNDERSTANDING DEPRESSION

How do I know if I'm depressed?

Everyone gets sad, blue, "down," and discouraged sometimes. For a few minutes, a few hours, or even a few days, things look pretty bleak. You might feel low in energy, tired, unable to concentrate, worried, or simply "flat"—as if you don't care about anything. Maybe you don't sleep well, or sleep more than usual but still feel tired. You may not feel like being with people, and you probably snarl at anyone who comes your way. Or maybe you cry more easily. You feel like nothing is going to work out, that you might as well crawl into a hole and give up.

But the feeling fades, and things get back on track later that day or the next day. Maybe whatever happened to make you feel that way doesn't seem so bad after all, or something else happens to cheer you up.

That's not what doctors mean when they talk about depression, or clinical depression. It is called "clinical depression" when you feel that way every day for a few weeks or more, and you don't feel any better even when good things happen. Depression affects your emotions, your thoughts, and even your body—and it doesn't feel good.

Who's depressed?

About one in five people gets depressed before the age of 20. This is a lot more than most people would guess! At any time, about 5% to 8% of young people will be depressed. That usually means a couple of people in any class at any time. Of course, people get better from depression, so next year it might be different kids. But there will always be a few.

A lot of the time, young people don't realize what is happening to them. They know they feel awful, but they can't explain what's happening. And often parents or teachers don't realize either. They might notice that the young person is very unhappy. But often nobody even notices that.

What is depression?

Depression is a very unpleasant emotional and physical state. People who are depressed feel sad or unhappy most of the time, even when good things are happening, and they feel physically unwell in many ways. Depression isn't just one thing. It isn't just being unhappy or tired or

One in five people gets depressed before the age of 20

not sleeping. It's a whole cluster of symptoms. It is called a "clinical depression" when at least five of these things happen together, most of the time, for at least two weeks:

- depressed or irritable mood   } one of these
- loss of interest in most things   } <u>must</u> be present
- insomnia or oversleeping
- loss of appetite, overeating, or weight gain
- fatigue or loss of energy
- physical and mental agitation or slowing down
- lack of concentration or indecisiveness
- feelings of worthlessness or guilt
- recurrent thoughts of death or suicide

The medical term for this is Major Depressive Episode. When people get a milder form of depression that goes on for a year or more, it is called Minor Depression, or Dysthymic Disorder.

Notice that there is a pattern of opposite symptoms. Two people experiencing depression may feel and look different from each other in many ways. One person may be very tired, sleep a lot, feel slowed down, and eat more. Another may feel agitated, pace around, not sleep, not eat, and have upsetting speedy thoughts. Yet they both have a form of clinical depression.

When you feel sad, irritable, and tired for a long time, things usually don't go well in your life. Depression affects how you get along with your family and friends, how you feel about yourself, your school work, and your ability to enjoy the things you usually do. And when your life doesn't go well, the depression itself gets worse. You can feel pretty hopeless.

Could I have something else?

The formal diagnosis of clinical depression needs to be made by a professional. Many counselors, social workers, and therapists as well as doctors, psychiatrists, and psychologists are trained to recognize these symptoms. But you will be asked to see your doctor to make sure something else is not causing your problem. For example, an infection, a hormonal problem, or other physical illnesses can cause similar symptoms.

What did I do to deserve this?

Nothing. Depression is your body's reaction to certain kinds of mental and physical stress happening over a long period of time. It is not your fault, or anyone else's. There are many causes of depression, as you will discover, but what they have in common is that they lead to discouragement. And discouragement is the starting point for depression.

Sometimes people who are depressed start blaming themselves. They think if they just "tried harder" they would feel better. Other times, family members or teachers say, "You just have a bad attitude." Depression is not an attitude. It is not something you can change just because you decide to. However, with some help and some work on your own, you can get better.

Lots of people have more stress than I have. Why me?

It is true that depression is just one possible reaction to stress. You may get depressed because you have inherited a tendency to depression. This is much like inheriting a tendency to being tall, having red hair, having diabetes, or getting ulcers. You may have relatives who have had depression—parents, siblings, grandparents, aunts or uncles.

Certain kinds of stress experienced over a long time can also cause depression. Stresses like learning problems, extreme worrying, emotional or physical abuse, parents breaking up, and other family problems may have gone on so long, day after day, that you started to believe things would never get better. You may have spent all your energy coping, or you got too discouraged to cope effectively. You may have lost confidence in your ability to handle things.

What kinds of stress cause depression?

There are some kinds of stresses that make young people more likely to get depressed. Being sick a lot or frequent moves and changes of school can make life more difficult and discouraging. We also know that having your parents break up and the death of relatives are two big stresses that can make you depressed. These are

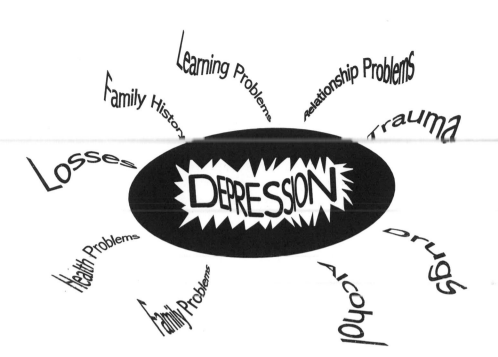

situations that feel out of your control. Even though they affect you, you can't do much to fix them. Often depression happens after you have had many upsetting things happen one after another. They added up to such a big load that you ran out of coping reserves, and one final disappointment or hurtful experience triggers the depression.

Can I get depressed without stress?

Depression can come on without any stress. This happens most often when there is a history of depression in your family, especially manic-depression, which we call "bipolar" because it has both highs and lows. Depression can also happen because of a viral illness or an imbalance in the thyroid or other key hormones. Depression can be caused by certain medicines you might take for other illnesses.

One of the commonest physical causes of depression people often forget to mention is alcohol. It is one of the most powerful depressant substances around. So are some other recreational drugs. Could one of them be causing your depression? Although some people think of marijuana as harmless, we know that people can get depressed on this drug.

Causes of Depression

- inherited risk, runs in the family
- experiences of abuse or abandonment
- parents fighting or separating
- family conflict
- learning problems
- attention deficit disorder
- chronic anxiety
- medical illness
- a recent loss or rejection in a relationship
- substance abuse

I feel sick. How can this be in my mind?

Depression is not just mental, it's physical. That's why physical things like sleep are disturbed. Some people can't fall asleep, and when they do, they wake up often. Even after sleeping, they feel exhausted in the morning. Some people find their sleep pattern is reversed, so that they sleep in the day and are up at night. Other people sleep more than 12 hours and still feel exhausted.

Appetite may be affected in the same way. Some people don't feel like eating at all. Others eat all the time and never feel satisfied. Still others crave certain food such as sweets and chocolate. Some people start binge eating during a time when they are depressed, and then can't stop afterward.

Depression causes all kinds of aches and pains: stomachaches, headaches, muscle tension aches. You can feel like you have some kind of flu virus. It can make you feel exhausted all the time.

Many people with depression don't believe they are depressed. Because they feel so sick, they think there must be something physically wrong, that it can't be in their head. And they are right: it isn't. Depression is very physical as well as mental. That's why it sometimes takes medicine, not just a psychological treatment, to get better.

Is there a test for depression?

There isn't any lab test for depression, although someday there might be. A medical doctor, psychiatrist, psychologist, or trained mental health counselor can tell from talking to you and hearing about your symptoms. The set of rules or criteria for accurately diagnosing depression were listed earlier on page 5.

There are also some rating scales for depression symptoms that may be used to help figure out how depressed you are, or to compare how you are feeling as you get better. It can also be helpful for the doctor or counselor to talk to your parents or teacher to get a clearer picture of how long this has been going on, and how things were before you got depressed. Often it is hard for people who are depressed to give a clear perspective because they are so lost in feeling depressed right now. They forget that they ever felt any different.

What kinds of depression are there?

One of the first things that needs to be sorted out is what kind of depression you have. Different kinds respond better to different treatments. Besides the "agitated" or "slowed down" types of depressions discussed earlier, there are other kinds. These are important to diagnose because they respond very well to certain specific treatments. Examples of these depressions are:

Seasonal Depression, or Seasonal Affective Disorder. This occurs in the wintertime. You feel like you are getting ready for hibernation. You feel very tired and sleep a lot. You also have a craving for sweets, which usually causes weight gain. This can be treated not only with medication but also with light. You sit beside a special kind of bright light for at least half an hour a day in the morning.

Bipolar Disorder, or Manic-Depression. This kind has different cycles or phases, from high (manic) to low (depressed). The high phase is the opposite of depression. You feel full of energy, on top of the world, and have unrealistic grandiose ideas. People get themselves into terrible trouble during a manic episode. They often lose touch with reality. They may spend money they don't have or become very reckless. Bipolar disorder is treated with medication and regulating your life.

Atypical Depression. This is a common form of depression in which people actually do cheer up a bit in reaction to things around them. They may also feel much more depressed when upsetting things happen. Being extrasensitive to being rejected is part of this kind of depression. Usually you sleep a lot and gain weight, as in seasonal depression, but not just in the wintertime. People with atypical depression usually feel the worst in the evening. Medications are effective for this kind of depression. It can also respond to psychological treatments.

Melancholic Depression. This is a much less common, very severe form of depression. You have loss of appetite, weight loss, severe concentration problems, and irrational guilt feelings. You feel worst first thing in the morning. You also wake up very early in the morning and are unable to fall back asleep. This kind of depression interferes greatly with your ability to function. In fact, people feel quite paralyzed by this depression and are unable to think about anything else. It needs to be treated with medication and does not get better with counseling or psychotherapy alone.

2.

GAINING CONTROL

So how do I get out of the pits?

The first step is to figure out what caused your depression. What are your stresses now and in the past? What is your usual coping style? What is your family history? What coping patterns did you learn from your parents? Are there any traumatic experiences that really added to your sense of discouragement? What's happening with your family, your school, and your friends right now? These are the kinds of things your doctor or counselor will ask you about.

Having figured out what kinds of things caused your depression, you can more easily figure out how to dig out of it. The treatment might include talking things through, making changes at home and school, learning some new ways to cope, or even medicine to deal with the physical parts of the depression.

The good news is that depression does get better. Most people are better in a few months. Some kinds of depression go on longer and are more resistant. But everyone eventually gets better.

Do I need therapy to get better?

Psychotherapy or counseling can really help depression. But it probably won't be like what some people imagine: lying on a couch for hours talking to a psychiatrist who doesn't say much. No one is going to read your mind either. Most talking therapies are very practical. They can even be enjoyable. You get to talk with someone who understands what is happening. You can figure out what caused your depression and how to get your life back on track. It is like a self-exploration with the help of a trained professional.

The person you talk to could be a counselor, a social worker, a nurse, a doctor, a psychologist, or a psychiatrist. Psychotherapy gives you a chance to talk to someone who really listens to your views. Together with your therapist, you can figure out how you feel, how you came to feel this way, and how to change your thinking or coping so that you get can out of the pits. Or together you might decide that some major changes need to be made in your family or school. Your therapist can help you figure out how to make that happen.

Sometimes, the best way to get out of depression is through attending a regular therapy group with other young people.

Can I take a pill to get over this?

It would be nice if it were so easy. Some kinds of depression are best treated with psychological and environmental changes instead of medication. Others are best treated with medicine. Many kinds are best treated with both.

Medication does speed up the healing process, but it still takes three to six weeks for the initial effects, and a few more weeks for the full effect. Most medications have some nuisance side effects which you may have to put up with while you are waiting to get better. But they do work.

Antidepressant medications are described in more detail later. But it is important to keep in mind that research on depression tells us that the best results are achieved with a combination of medication and some form of talking therapy.

Do I need to be hospitalized?

Most young people with depression do not need to be hospitalized. But there are some situations in which hospitalization is a good idea. If you are so depressed that you don't eat at all, or your physical health is suffering, you may need to start treatment in the hospital. If you are so suicidal and hopeless that it is unsafe for you to be at home, hospitalization would be necessary. Another reason is if the type of depression is very hard to treat and further investigation or specialized treatment is recommended.

Usually people are kept in the hospital as little time as possible. Just being in the hospital doesn't necessarily speed up getting better, and it takes you away from your friends and the things in your life you can enjoy. Most people are more comfortable in their own homes with their own belongings. Besides, it may be important to work on changing some things at home or in your life, and it is better to do that on the spot. Occasionally, however, the home situation is so unhealthy that it is better to be out of it for a while, while the depression gets sorted out.

Should I go to school when I'm depressed?

This can be a difficult decision. It is something you should talk over with your doctor or therapist. Usually, it is best to go to school and to try to keep things moving in your life. Otherwise you get further behind, and more and more isolated from other people. However, it is hard to keep going to school if your concentration is not good and if you are feeling depressed and irritable. You may find it hard to learn things in class. You may not feel like talking to your friends.

It helps if someone at school understands what is going on with you. Maybe you or your parents can talk to the school counselor. The counselor can help you figure out some ways to adjust things at school so you can manage better. Sometimes the amount of work you do can be cut down for a while. Or you may need some extra help to catch up. It may be a good idea to drop a course you don't need, to give you more time to work on

You may need extra support to get through school.

the important ones. There are plenty of solutions available. But you need to explore them with someone who can support you. And you need a plan.

If depression goes on for a long time and really gets in the way of schoolwork, there are some other possibilities. One is attending a special smaller class for a while, where you can get more help and there is less stress on you. In some places, there is a "day treatment" program where you not only get to do your schoolwork but also get personal and group counseling.

Together with your school, your family, and a mental

health professional, you can figure out what is the best approach for you. It is important to have a plan that works. The plan is not working if you find yourself staying home in bed. If that happens, the plan needs to be revised. You need to be active and involved with people to get over depression. In that sense, it is like a muscle injury which needs to be exercised gently to prevent stiffness. Most times, you feel better when you are with other young people, and when you are accomplishing things. If you become too inactive, any little thing becomes a big effort because your coping muscles are out of shape.

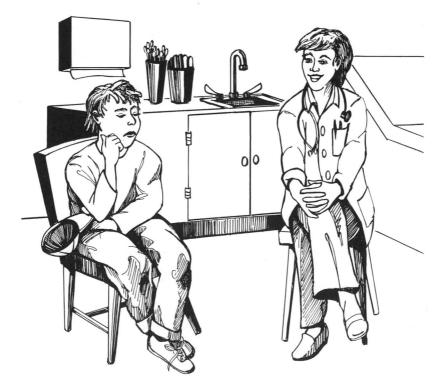

3.

HELPING YOURSELF

What can I do to help myself?

There is a lot you can do to help yourself. Here are some tips to help prevent depression, and to help you get better faster:

- get regular sleep, food, and exercise
- keep a balance between work and play
- do hobbies and physical activities
- hang out with people who bring you up, not down
- organize your schoolwork and do it in steady bits
- use resource people
- don't let things mushroom
- keep track of your successes
- make a plan

Exercise

Exercise helps depression in several ways. Research shows that it directly affects the brain chemicals involved in depression. You have also probably heard of the "natural high" that people get from exercise because of the

Keeping active and being with friends are ways to feel better.

brain chemicals called "endorphins." The trick is finding an activity that you like to do. There is no use trying to go running every day if you really hate running. You may enjoy walking the dog or going swimming. It is more helpful if the exercise is more vigorous than walking, but something is better than nothing.

Exercise improves your energy, improves your sleep, and may improve your mood. It is a good idea to make a deal to exercise regularly with a friend or a family member. This makes it more fun, and helps you get going when you don't feel like it.

Sleep

Problems with sleeping too much (hypersomnia) or being unable to sleep (insomnia) are common with depression. Improving them may also relieve your depression. You will certainly be less stressed if you sleep better.

If you are having trouble falling asleep, try getting into a routine of settling to sleep at the same time each night. This helps set your biological clock, which is often out of kilter in depression. Have a warm bath. Drink some warm milk or chamomile tea with a few not-too-sweet cookies or some cheese and crackers. Then settle down to read something, not too exciting, until you get tired. Then turn off the light. If you find yourself thinking or worrying instead of sleeping, try listening to some calming music or do a relaxation exercise. Imagine a favorite calm place, such as a warm beach on a sunny day. Close your eyes and imagine drifting off to sleep in the warmth. If you remain wide awake, sit up or get up into a chair and read for a while longer, until you feel sleepy again. Watching TV is not a good idea, because it is hard to tear yourself away from it even if you do get sleepy.

The same things can help if you wake up in the night a lot. The main thing that keeps people awake during the night is worrying about the fact that they aren't falling asleep! Unfortunately, you cannot will yourself to sleep.

The harder you try, the more wide awake you are. You need to distract yourself from this concern, and eventually you will probably fall asleep.

For some kinds of depression, the sleep problem simply will not go away until the depression gets better. Even sleeping pills don't work. In this situation, an antidepressant medication usually works, but it may take a few weeks. Occasionally, a sedative will be prescribed for a short time until the antidepressant works.

One surprising treatment for sleep problems is "sleep deprivation." You deliberately stay up for either an entire night or just the last half of the night. As long as you don't go to sleep until the next evening at the normal time, without napping during the day, this can dramatically relieve depression. The relief may be short-lived, but it can speed up the response to an antidepressant, and it sometimes does improve the sleep pattern greatly for the next week or two. The reason this works is that sleep deprivation resets the biological clock. In some cases, it seems to effectively restabilize this internal clock, which is disrupted in a depressive episode. Talk this idea over with your doctor before trying it on your own.

If your problem is oversleeping, it is important to find some way of getting up in the morning. By getting up at a regular time, you can help set your biological clock. Generally, sleeping 12 or more hours does not relieve depression, and it may make it worse. This is a situation in which sleep deprivation can help as a treatment to reset the clock. Sleep deprivation also tends to have an antidepressant effect.

Your problem might be "sleep reversal." This is when

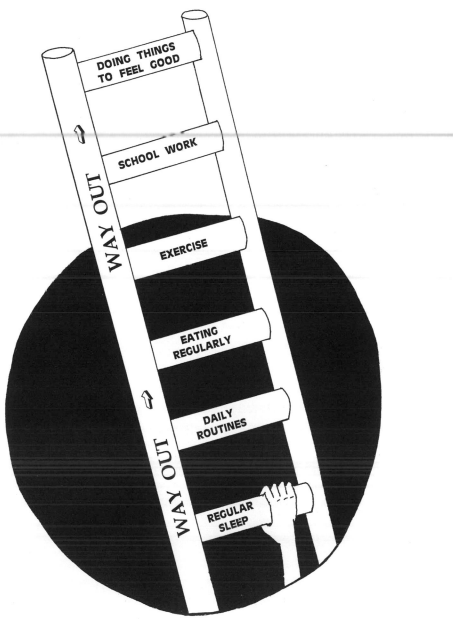

Getting Out of the Pit

your internal clock shifts later each day so that you fall asleep at 2:00 a.m., then 3:00 a.m., then 4:00 a.m. Eventually, you sleep in the daytime and are awake at night. This pattern can worsen depression. It certainly makes life difficult. You miss school and end up alone at night while everyone else is sleeping. Of course, when you are depressed, you might like this pattern because it allows you to avoid seeing people!

The main way to avoid sleep reversal is to keep getting up early in the morning. It is less important when you go to bed, because the time you get up sets the internal clock. Again, because it is hard to push yourself to get up early once you get into this pattern, the sleep deprivation technique can help. Because things tend to creep around the clock again, you may need to do this once a month or so if the problem persists. If this occurs mostly in the wintertime, morning light therapy is also a strategy.

If your sleep problems persist, you could benefit from a consultation with a sleep disorders specialist. Your doctor may also suggest sleeping pills temporarily, while you are being treated for depression. Be sure to ask whether you are supposed to take them every day or only after a few bad nights of sleep, because some of these medications are habit forming.

Daily routines

Setting up regular daily routines relieves depression in several ways. First, it keeps you going when your energy

Weekly Calendar from _____ to _____

	SUNDAY	MONDAY	TUESDAY
9:00			
10:00		remember English project.	
11:00	friends within		
12:00	math homework		
1:00			
2:00			
3:00	-meet Sam at mall		
4:00		swimming	basketball practice
5:00	study for math quiz		
6:00	dinner	dinner	dinner
7:00	T.V.	homework	go to library for project
8:00		phone calls	
9:00		finish homework	phone calls
10:00		T.V.	homework
	get to bed!	to bed!	to bed

and motivation are low. It takes less effort to get going if your routines are predictable and don't take a lot of thought. Second, you have a sense of being organized and getting somewhere despite not feeling good. Third, routines are needed to develop sleep and exercise habits. Make sure that your routines include time for friends, relaxation, fun, and exercise, as well as homework and regular eating.

It is a good idea to make a big calendar or poster of your routine and hang it in your bedroom, kitchen, family room—wherever you are most likely to see it.

Eating regularly

It sounds obvious to eat regularly, but when people are depressed they often don't feel hungry or just can't be bothered. Not eating makes your energy and concentration much worse. It is important not only to eat regularly but to consider what you actually eat. You need to eat breakfast; otherwise you are running on stress chemicals all morning and tend to crave sugar. The sugar gives you energy, but a few hours later, your blood sugar drops dramatically and you feel tired and irritable. Then you crave more sugar, and the vicious cycle continues.

Instead, you need to choose foods that stay with you, that are not too sweet, and that cover the "basic food groups." These include fruit and vegetables, cereals and bread, and meat, fish, eggs, or alternative protein sources. This is not just because this is what your mother said is "good for you." You actually need very specific protein building blocks and vitamins to make the brain chemicals (serotonin, noradrenaline, and others) you need to recover from depression. Antidepressants also need these building blocks to work.

Eating well will improve your energy and concentration and will allow you to recover successfully from depression.

School work

When you are depressed, it is hard to tackle your work. Everything seems monumental and impossible. You think that it is no use trying because your effort won't be good enough anyway.

The best way to handle school work is to break it up into small chunks and tackle it one piece at a time. Making a detailed schedule can help. Work for short bits, congratulate yourself while you take a break, and then do a bit more. Eventually you will begin to see progress. You may not be able to concentrate for as long as usual, so don't try to work as long at a stretch.

When you get so far behind you don't know where to start, try getting a tutor or someone else to sit down with you. A study period at school can help you get homework done when you are fresher in the daytime. The study period may have a resource or support teacher who can help you get organized if you are feeling overwhelmed.

You can try making a deal with a good friend to call to encourage you to get started on half an hour of homework, and then call you again at the end for a chat break before you do the next bit. This could help both of you.

If you need other ideas about handling school work, the best person to talk to is usually your school coun-

Having some fun helps, too.

selor who is trained in study skills and knows what other resources are available in your school.

Doing what makes you feel good

When you are feeling depressed, you often forget the things that might make you feel better. It might be a favorite piece of music, watching a comedy show, going for a walk in the park, having a soothing bath. It might be talking on the phone to people who make you feel better, as opposed to those who bring you down. It might be certain colors of clothes or reading a certain author.

Make a list of things that make you feel good, even a

little bit. You can hang a copy on your wall or keep it with you in your notebook (or both). Then, when you are feeling down, you can look at it to see what you can try. Also, building more of these things into your daily routine can make you feel better overall.

What do I do when I feel like giving up?

Many people feel that way sometimes. In fact, studies show that at least one in eight young people thought about suicide at some point in the past year. But feeling that way occurs much more often, and much more intensely, when you are depressed. When you get discouraged, you lose perspective, and things seem too hard. Going to sleep forever or stopping the world starts to look pretty appealing. It's no solution. And thinking that way tends to interfere with doing things that will make a difference. There are plenty of solutions, but feeling suicidal is a sign that you are feeling stuck, and you can't think of them right now, or they seem to take more energy than you have available.

If you start feeling like you can't carry on, tell someone. Just telling your friends isn't good enough. They are going to be put in a hard position, since they will have to tell an adult because they care about you and want to make sure you are safe. So you also need to talk to your parents, your doctor, or other adults. If no one is around, call a crisis line or go to the nearest hospital emergency department.

Other people can help you.

When you feel suicidal, you've lost perspective, and you need help to regain it. Things will get better, but you need help to get from here to there. Help is out there.

Can I get over this on my own?

Maybe. But why make things so hard for yourself? The most powerful antidepressant around is action—positive, powerful, problem-solving kinds of action. But when you're depressed, it's hard to get that going on your own. That's where help comes in. Other people can help you mobilize your own resources to make a difference.

You *will* get better. But your recovery is faster, more complete, and more permanent with good help. Besides, being depressed and alone is even worse than being depressed. So tell someone. Ask for help.

Does this mean I'm always going to be a weak person?

Not at all. In fact, people who learn to deal with stress and depression in their teen years may be in better shape to deal with stresses later in life because they know themselves better and have some new skills. But getting depressed knocks the confidence out of you, so you might need some time and help to build that back up. That's why trying to pretend it isn't happening doesn't make sense. Facing depression straight on gives you a chance to get something out of a lousy experience.

Where do I get help?

Start with someone who knows what they are doing: your doctor, your school counselor, a psychologist, a child and adolescent psychiatrist, or people at a mental health center. If you are stuck, call a crisis line or hospital, and they will tell you where to find help. Start somewhere, and people will help you through the process of getting the right kind of help.

4.
MEDICATION

Depression is very physical. Even if it was triggered by psychological stresses, it eventually affects your body. Sometimes, the physical symptoms can be resolved with psychological treatment. However, your doctor may also suggest an antidepressant medication. Here are some things you will want to know about how they work.

Brain chemicals

When people are depressed, changes occur in their brain and body chemicals. The medicines that work on brain chemicals to help depression are called "antide-pressants." They are not stimulants or "uppers." They do not make you happier than normal if you are not depressed. What we think they do is to rebuild chemicals in the brain that are depleted by stress or by an inborn imbalance. These brain chemicals include serotonin, noradrenaline, and sometimes dopamine. They are involved in regulating emotions, activity, thinking, sleeping, and eating.

Mind-body connection

Animal studies have shown that animals can get something that looks a lot like depression if they are put in frustrating situations over which they have no control. We call this condition "learned helplessness." It results in the same kinds of physical changes that happen in depressed people. And antidepressants make it better. What this research tells us is that your body and mind are connected. What happens in your mind affects your body chemistry. And what happens in your body chemistry affects your mind and your emotions.

Cautions

Antidepressants take a while to work. All antidepressants take several weeks to work fully, while the side effects often occur in the first few days. Keep in touch with your doctor to discuss concerns you have about potential side effects, and your response to the medicine.

Check before mixing medications. Be sure to check with your doctor or pharmacist before combining these medicines with other prescriptions. Also, do not mix them with alcohol or drugs. Ask your doctor for some advice if you anticipate that this will be a problem for you.

Don't stop antidepressants suddenly. Many antidepressants have withdrawal effects, so you need to taper them slowly, and with your doctor's advice, before stopping. Also, don't stop them too soon. This is like finishing the whole antibiotic prescription so the infection won't come back. Most of the time, antidepressants should be continued for at least six to nine months before you taper off carefully.

Antidepressants don't work alone. Antidepressants should be always be combined with other treatment approaches, including changes in coping behavior and environment.

Classes of antidepressants

There are four main kinds of antidepressants: tricyclics, SSRIs, MAOIs, and "novel" or different antidepressants. Here is some information about each of them. Each type has its advantages and disadvantages. Your doctor should decide with you which kind makes the most sense for you. Notice that most of the antidepressants can work well for other symptoms, like panic attacks and migraine headaches. Some of the antidepressants also help other problems, such as attention deficit hyperactivity disorder. If you have one of these other problems, that could be a guide to which antidepressant to choose.

Tricyclic Antidepressants

- imipramine (Tofranil[R]), amitriptyline
- desipramine (Norpramin[R], Pertorfane[R])
- nortriptyline (Aventyl[R])
- clomipramine (Anafranil[R])

What are they used for?
- clinical depression
- panic disorder
- other forms of anxiety, such as separation anxiety, phobias
- attention deficit disorder (imipramine, desipramine, nortriptyline)
- obsessive-compulsive disorder (clomipramine only)
- sleep disturbances
- eating disorders
- chronic pain
- migraine headaches

How do they work? Tricyclic antidepressants increase the effects of brain chemicals (serotonin and noradrenaline) involved in mood, anxiety, and biological regulation of sleep, activity, attention, and arousal levels.

What are the side effects? These are strong medicines, and they do have side effects. This is why they are reserved for some of the more serious forms of depres-

Your doctor may suggest an antidepressant.

sion, or if depression occurs with other problems, such as attention deficit disorder, obsessive-compulsive disorder, and sometimes panic attacks. Most of the side effects are not serious, but at high doses, these medicines can be toxic, so they must be monitored by a doctor. Your doctor may want to get an electrocardiogram (ECG), which is a tracing of your heart's electrical activity, to make sure that your heart is not sensitive to the higher doses of these medicines.

- most side effects improve with time
- several tricyclics cause drowsiness, so they are given in the evening
- common nuisance effects: dry mouth, blurred vision, constipation
- occasional effects: queasy stomach or nausea, allergic rashes
- low blood pressure on standing up, helped by getting up slowly, drinking more water
- increase in heart rate
- at high doses or toxic levels: heart rhythm problems

Note: These medications are poisonous and can cause death in overdose! Keep out of reach of children. Daily prescribed dose must not be exceeded, and these medicines should not be stopped suddenly, or without your doctor's advice, because withdrawal effects occur.

How long do they take to work? Because brain chemicals are being restored, there is little change for the first week or two, and then response is gradual over 4-6 weeks. The medication should be continued for a period of at least 6 months to firmly establish the improvement in mood or anxiety. It should be used longer for chronic anxiety or attentional problems.

Specific Serotonin Reuptake Inhibitors (SSRIs)

- fluoxetine (Prozac^R)
- fluvoxamine (Luvox^R)

- paroxetine (Paxil[R])
- sertraline (Zoloft[R])

Related serotoninergic medications
- nefazadone (Serzone[R])
- trazodone (Desyrel[R])
- buspirone (Buspar[R])

What are they used for?
- clinical depression
- panic disorder
- other anxiety disorders
- obsessive compulsive disorder
- eating disorders
- premenstrual mood disorders
- migraine headaches
- other special clinical uses

What are the side effects?
- very few, rarely serious
- minor side effects improve in the first week
- nuisance side effects: upset stomach, headache
- some SSRIs are sedative, while others are more activating (e.g., fluoxetine)
- rare: allergic reactions, as with any drug

This group of antidepressants is now the most commonly prescribed for young people. This is because of their safety, low side effects, and general effectiveness.

How do they work? They increase the effects of serotonin, a brain chemical that regulates mood, anxiety, sleep, appetite, and activity. The altered level of serotonin relieves the depressive symptoms.

How long do they take to work? There is little change for the first week or two, then gradual improvement over 3-6 weeks. Usually energy or sleep improves first, but your mood doesn't get better for a few weeks. The medication is continued for about 6 months, while mood or anxiety is stabilized, or longer for chronic conditions or recurrent depression.

Monoamine Oxidase Inhibitors (MAOIs)

This is an interesting and very effective group of antidepressants, which are not used often because of the potentially very severe, even life-threatening side effects if you don't follow the prescribed diet. They do, however, work very specifically in atypical depression. That is the kind mentioned earlier, with excessive sleeping, excessive eating, and sensitivity to rejection. There is a new member of this class, a "reversible" MAOI, which is safe and does not require dietary restrictions but may not be quite as effective. These medicines, except for moclobemide, are usually reserved for treatment-resistant depression.

- phenelzine (Nardil[R])
- tranylcypromine (Parnate[R])

newer "reversible" MAOI:

- moclobemide (Manerix[R])

What are they used for?
- clinical depression
- panic disorder
- social phobia
- eating disorders

What are the side effects? The older MAOIs require dietary restrictions to prevent a very serious side effect: extremely high blood pressure due to an interaction with the chemical tyramine found in some foods. Moclobemide has few side effects, and usually requires no dietary restriction except at very high doses.

How do they work? They prevent the breakdown of the brain chemicals serotonin and noradrenaline, restoring normal neurotransmitter levels and regulating mood and anxiety.

Novel Antidepressants

These antidepressants don't fit into the other classes and often have a special profile of action. Newer antidepressants are being created all the time, to try to get the best effect with as few side effects as possible.

- venlafaxine (Effexor[R])—strong antidepressant with similar effects to tricyclics but different and less serious side effects

- trazodone (Desyrel[R])—very sedative, so of limited use; helpful for sleep problems in depression
- nefazodone (Serzone[R])—related to trazodone, less sedative
- bupropion (Wellbutrin[R])—entirely different, stimulating medication that works in some kinds of severe depression or depressive phase of bipolar disorder, also for attention deficit hyperactivity disorder

Mood Stabilizers

- lithium
- carbamazepine
- valproic acid

What are they used for? We now recognize that more people have a mild form of bipolar disorder than we used to think. Some respond best to mood stabilizers, rather than antidepressants, when they are depressed as well as when they are in the manic phase.

What are the side effects? All three mood stabilizers have various nuisance effects, such as drowsiness and weight gain. All three need to have levels adjusted based on blood tests, because too low a dose is ineffective, while too high a dose can be poisonous. The blood tests can be a bother. But once the right dose is found, they don't need to be done often. They are also very effective treatments, and young people can feel quite comfortable on them.

What if the first medicine doesn't work?

About 70-80% of the time, the first medicine will work very well. Sometimes it may need to be "boosted" by another medication. Other times it turns out that a person simply responds better to a different class of medicine, so if one doesn't work well, another class will be chosen after a good trial of at least 6 weeks of the first medicine.

Remember that it takes weeks to feel better, and often the last thing to get better is how you feel inside. It's hard to be patient, so you need lots of support during the waiting period.

Other treatments

As mentioned earlier, "seasonal" or winter depression can respond to an intense light for about half an hour every morning. You have to keep using the light every day during the winter to keep up the good effects. Some other kinds of depression may also be helped by light therapy.

Very severe depression may respond best to electro-convulsive therapy, or ECT. How this works is to dramatically and suddenly, through electrical stimulation of the brain, raise the levels of those brain chemicals we've been talking about. Done with a very brief general anesthetic, this has become such a quick and effective treatment that it can now be done without people having to stay in the hospital overnight. While this may seem a drastic treatment, it is more rapidly effective than the antidepressants, so that patients who are suffering intensely with severe or treatment-resistant depression may be offered this to resolve the episode more quickly.

Things to remember

Mixing alcohol or street drugs with antidepressants is definitely not a good idea. In fact, it is guaranteed to make your depression worse. If you have trouble with this, you need to talk to your counselor or doctor about it. There is help for this problem.

Some antidepressants can have an effect on a developing fetus. It is important to avoid pregnancy until you are off the medication. This means practicing some kind of birth control if you are sexually active. Talk to your doctor about this.

Do not stop an antidepressant suddenly. If you do, you can feel very sick, throw up, and have chills and headaches. If it is time to stop your medication, your doctor will explain to you how to taper it slowly.

Antidepressants are not addictive, but you do need to stay on them long enough to keep depression from coming back. Your doctor will make a plan with you for how long this should be. It is often a good idea to wait until the summer to stop a medication so your schoolwork won't suffer if depression does start to come back.

Remember that there are things you can do for yourself that can also have a chemical antidepressant effect. These include exercise, eating regularly, and making an effort to stay in contact with friends.

5.

PSYCHOTHERAPY

What is psychotherapy?

Psychotherapy is a general name for psychological therapies used for emotional problems like depression or anxiety. The main idea behind these treatments is that by exploring your concerns, talking about them, thinking about them in new ways, and learning new ways of responding and behaving, your emotional problems will get better.

There are many different styles of psychotherapy. Some work better for one person or for one kind of depression. You may have to try one out to see how it suits you. Therapy may done with you individually or in a group. In some cases, very effective therapy is done with the whole family.

What kinds of therapy are there?

If we listed all the kinds of psychotherapy, it would be a very long list. To name a few, there are cognitive therapy, behavioral therapy, psychoanalytic psychotherapy, interpersonal therapy, narrative therapy, supportive psychotherapy, social skills training, family therapy, art therapy, and music therapy. Within each of these kinds, there are many subtypes.

Why are there so many kinds of therapy? Mainly because different styles work better with different people. And certain kinds of therapy work better with certain kinds of depression. Also, therapists may work better with styles of treatment that suit their personality type.

For your information, here are some features and strategies of different psychotherapies. Many therapists combine these theories and strategies, depending on what seems most helpful at a particular time.

Supportive Therapy or Counseling. This focuses on hearing out your concerns and helping you to decide how to handle things more effectively. You might be given some practical advice on taking better care of yourself, or on ways to talk to your parents more effectively, or on how to deal with school. The counselor acts as a coach or encourager.

Stress Management Training. This offers tools for handling stress better. It includes tips about eating, sleeping, and exercising regularly and avoiding alcohol and drugs. It also includes time management and specific techniques for relaxing your mind and body.

Social Skills and Assertiveness Training. This provides ways of managing problems with other people,

Psychotherapy makes a big difference.

including how to make and keep friends, how to let people know you are not happy with something, and how to get your point across effectively. Even if you had pretty good social skills before getting depressed, depression often knocks down your confidence. So you may need to brush up on some of these tools to rebuild it.

Cognitive-Behavioral Therapy. This type of treatment is based on the idea that negative ways of thinking and acting make you more depressed. For example, if you are always thinking, "Nobody ever likes me," this can lead you to not bother to call people up, or not bother to try to make friends. You may walk around your school without looking at anybody, which signals that you don't want to be talked to. So no one talks to you, and you conclude that no one likes you. It gets to be a vicious circle, what is called a "self-fulfilling prophesy." In other words, the prediction that things will go badly leads you to act in such a way that they really do go badly for you.

This thinking pattern is often associated with some faulty logic called "cognitive errors." Examples include: **Overgeneralization:** if one thing goes wrong, it proves everything will go wrong. **Catastrophization:** If my friend doesn't return my phone call, it means she doesn't like me, and if she doesn't like me, none of her friends like me, and if they don't like me, nobody at school likes me. If nobody at school likes me, nobody will ever like me. This example also shows another error: **Jumping to conclusions:** Maybe your friend didn't call you because she had too much homework to do, or someone else was tying up her phone.

These negative thinking habits are often learned from the bad experiences you've had in the past, most of which were not your fault. Sometimes, one of your parents thinks the same way and you learned it at home. Other times, just being depressed makes your thinking very negative and you get into a habit of it.

In cognitive-behavioral therapy, you identify the patterns of thinking you have, and test them out by experiments to see if they are as reasonable as they seemed to you. You practice different ways of behaving (for example, making experimental phone calls, making eye contact, and smiling in the hall at school) and eventually develop more balanced ways of thinking. Cognitive-behavioral therapy is definitely work, but it pays off.

Interpersonal Therapy. This is similar to cognitive therapy, but it focuses on some different aspects of relationships: role transitions, unresolved grief, and role disputes. You identify areas to work on that have to do with unresolved losses or on relationship difficulties, such as with your parents. You also look at how your way of relating doesn't get you what you want. The therapist helps you develop more effective solutions to reduce your isolation, loneliness, and frustration.

Psychodynamic or Exploratory Therapy. There are many approaches to what is called "psychodynamic" therapy. What they have in common is a focus on how unconscious ways of thinking and acting affect the way you experience things. Usually, things in your past, including traumas and losses, are explored as part of understanding why you may feel as you do in the present. This approach can be helpful in milder and chronic depression. But it can often be overwhelming to work on past experiences if you are very depressed, as you tend to dwell on negative events without being able to shake free of them.

Expressive, Art, and Music Therapies. These approaches include drawing, painting, drama, and other forms of creative expression. They may be helpful for people who have trouble getting in touch with their feel-

Art therapy can help you understand and express how you feel.

ings or talking about what bothers them. Usually, they are accompanied by some discussion of the feelings that are revealed and suggestions for ways of resolving them.

Family Therapy. Sometimes, working with the whole family is the best way to tackle depression. This is usually the case when ongoing problems in the family are contributing to the depression and prevent it from getting better. Examples are parents who are fighting a lot, a problem with favoritism, or serious clashes between siblings. Sometimes one of the parents has personal problems that affect everyone. Sometimes there has been a terrible grief no one has been able to talk about, like the loss of a child or a baby many years ago. Other times, the reason for working with the family is simply that the family's reaction to the depressed person is making the situation worse.

Many young people don't want their family involved. It is important to have a sense of privacy with a therapist. However, not involving the family may mean that other people don't change, and you take on the whole burden of change yourself. Sometimes that helps, but if there really is a problem in the family, it is better to tackle it directly. A combination of individual and family therapy is often helpful.

Group Therapy. Groups are often suggested for young people with depression. The group might have a focus of support, social skills, cognitive behavioral treatment, exploration, or a combination. The special advantages of groups are:

- You can learn from other people's experiences and solutions
- You do not feel so alone
- You can practice social and assertiveness skills
- You get ideas from people your own age
- You get encouragement from other young people
- It can be fun!

Some groups last a year or more, so you develop some trust and closeness with people who are not part of the rest of your life. You also get some pretty good feedback about your ways of handling things. Other groups focus on learning skills together rather than getting to know each other. One thing that is important in all groups is confidentiality. You need to know that people won't talk about your problems outside of the group.

Groups are often combined with some individual therapy and with medication.

Which kind is best?

The really interesting thing is that most of these therapies do work. But they often work for what we call "nonspecific" reasons. In other words, it is not the details of a specific therapy that work, but rather the therapeutic process, which all these therapies have in common. That means the relationship between you and the therapist, and the work you do together to sort things out. Some of the important nonspecific factors involved are a chance to express your feelings, a chance to be understood, a shared idea about what caused the problem in the first place, and shared ideas about what needs to be done to get things better. Simply put, if you and your therapist are on the same wavelength, and you feel understood, it is likely that the two of you will figure out some solutions. Research studies show that almost 90% of the effectiveness of different psychotherapies seems to be due to these nonspecific factors.

That doesn't mean that any treatment will work with anybody. In order for you to get that feeling of being understood, and to be on the same wavelength, the therapy style has to match your style. If you like to talk, talking about things might be best. If you have trouble talking about your feelings, art therapy might be helpful. If you know what you need to do, but are too stuck to get going on it, a cognitive-behavioral style might help build up skills to get you unstuck.

Finally, there is the personal connection between you and your therapist. You can't work with just anyone, even if they are well trained and very good at what they do. For therapy to work, there has to be a good personality match.

Remember that just as different medicines work better for different individuals, different kinds of psychotherapy and different therapists work better for different people. So don't give up if therapy doesn't work the first time. Remember as well that psychotherapy, like antidepressant medicines, takes time. Things don't get better right away. There may even be a few side effects. First, you have to work hard to make some changes. Second, some of those changes may be resisted by people around you who are used to having you the old, depressed way. But this work really pays off!

Goals of Psychotherapy

- to help you get out of an episode of depression
- to help prevent depression from coming back
- to teach you some new skills
- to give you the experience of being understood and supported while you talk about your feelings and experiences
- to encourage you to use your own resources to solve problems more effectively

6.

AFTER THE DEPRESSION

What do I do next?

Depression does not last forever. One way or another, it will get better. One of the things we know from research on depression in young people is that, like other illnesses or injuries, depression leaves "scars." After a bad flu virus, it takes a while to rebuild your energy. After an injury, it takes a while to rebuild your flexibility and strength. After a blow to your confidence, it takes a while to get up the nerve to try things again. Depression is like having all those things at once. Your physical energy, your confidence, and your patterns of doing things all get disrupted. It takes a while to rebuild them all.

As you get better, it is important to think about your goals. Where would you like to be a few months from now? What kinds of activities do you want to do? What kinds of friends do you want to have? What are your school goals? The first step is to figure out where you want to get to, and then work on a plan. All of the ideas about exercise, eating well, sleep patterns, and having a good routine discussed in Chapter 2 will help.

Getting back with friends can be difficult—at first.

Will I still have friends?

When you are depressed, you may lose touch with your friends. When you don't feel like going out much, you often decline invitations or don't return phone calls. When you are feeling better, it is time to let people know that you want to be more involved again. Make some phone calls or join some activities. The drama club or yearbook committee at school might be a way to meet people. If you like sports, join a team or go to the pool or weight room where you can meet other young people with similar interests.

Sometimes you have to make a decision about friends. Maybe the people you were spending time with before you got depressed were not helping. Especially if they were into drug or alcohol use as a way of having fun, spending more time with them may bring you down again. Think about who is healthy and fun for you to be with, and try to spend time with those people.

Will I catch up in school?

When depression goes on for a while, it may have made you lose some time at school. You may even have to repeat part or all of a year. This can be discouraging. However, it is no different from what happens when people get pneumonia or have to have surgery. They may miss most of a term and simply not be able to make up the work because they are too ill. This is not anyone's fault.

You will catch up!

Will the depression return?

Unfortunately, there is at least a 50% chance that depression will come back at some time during your life. If it does happen, however, you'll know right away and be able to get help quickly. Also, putting into practice everything you've learned, or getting a medicine sooner, may make the depression go away faster.

Are there any good effects from depression?

Depression is an awful thing to go through, but there can be some positive effects after it is over. You will probably have learned a few things about yourself, as well as some ways of handling stress better. What you have learned may decrease the chance that you'll get depressed again. Your new coping abilities should help you in many areas of your life and make you a more resilient person.

Depression is tough—but it may teach you new coping abilities.

7.

OTHER PEOPLE'S STORIES

Here are two stories about how some other young people with depression have felt—just so you know you really are not alone in this.

Kevin's Story

It has been a terrible year. It seemed like I messed everything up. The football team. My school. My friends. My family.

I used to be a happy-go-lucky person. I played a lot of sports, went out with my friends, crammed for exams—swimming through life just like everyone else. Then, for no reason, I starting drowning. It felt like I was sinking, and there was nothing I could hold onto to keep myself above water.

I started sleeping all the time, but I still barely dragged myself out of bed. I fell asleep in class, couldn't remember anything, started failing my tests, argued with my parents, broke up with my girlfriend, quit the team, and crawled into a hole in my room and never wanted to come out again. All in a few weeks.

My world was coming apart, and I couldn't stop it. Worst of all, it seemed like it was all my fault. Everyone was disappointed in me—when I didn't remember my chores, when I didn't hand my essay in, when I slapped my sister Kate for bugging me a million times with her teasing, when I was late (again) for my first class in the morning. I couldn't seem to do anything right.

And after a while I didn't care anyway. I couldn't be bothered. When my math teacher got mad at me for not doing any homework, I just stared at him, and then I walked out of the class and kept walking out of the school. When my father yelled at me for sitting in front of the TV for hours instead of doing my work, I just walked out of the room, went to my bedroom, and slammed the door.

Sometimes I cried, but usually I just sat in the dark and did nothing. I started to feel scared—like I couldn't stand going on with my life anymore.

How did I get to that point? I never would have imagined it six months ago. I guess I'd been fed up and feeling down for a couple of months. Since the end of the summer. Nothing seemed fun anymore. I just didn't care about anything. I felt sick a lot of the time. I wish I knew how it all got started.

I did have mono last year. I got the sore throat, headaches, fevers, and felt very tired for a few weeks. I missed a lot of school, and then it was hard to go back. I missed almost a whole term of math. That's getting to me this year, because I missed stuff I still don't understand.

Some other things happened. My parents decided on a "trial separation" for a while last spring. They weren't getting along, and they thought it would be good for everyone if they had a break. "Speak for yourself," I muttered, but who would listen to me? My kid sisters and I had to shuttle back and forth between our house and my dad's apartment. Dad was so hurt when we didn't want to spend every weekend with him. Like I have time for that.

I was angry with both of them, and I started spending most of my time with my friends over the summer. The partying ones. My parents got mad because I was staying out so late, but nobody was in charge as far as I was concerned. They'd blown the family apart anyway, so I didn't care what they thought. So I drank a lot for a few months. That took my mind off a lot, but it wrecked me for school in the mornings when the fall came.

Then the bottom fell out of everything, and I wasn't even going to school half the time. Finally, one night my father blew up at me. The next morning, he came into my room and told me I had an appointment with our doctor. For some reason I felt very shaky, like something awful was going to happen.

I was in a daze when Dr. Mason was checking me over. I can't even remember what I said when he asked me questions. I sat there feeling stupid, with Dr. Mason looking at me with this serious expression.

After the checkup, he told me to come into the other part of his office with the big desk and the shelves of books. I sat down. He said we needed to talk. I felt my heart beating hard, and I couldn't find my voice. My eyes were watering and I became embarrassed. I wanted to run out of there, but that would be so stupid. Dr. Mason had known me for a long time, so what was I afraid of?

Dr. Mason asked how school was going. I said, Fine (a lie, of course). He asked if I was under too much pressure. It doesn't matter what I said because I don't even remember. Now I think I was very lucky because Dr. Mason understood even what I didn't say. When Dr. Mason asked me how I felt inside, I suddenly remembered about the drowning feeling. I told him I felt like I was sinking. I felt I wasn't alive inside anymore. I said I slept all the time, but it felt like I never slept. I had more friends than I ever had, but I felt like there was a miserable gray fog surrounding me. I couldn't "feel" my friends anymore. No matter how warm and friendly they were, I felt chilled and cold.

Dr. Mason leaned forward and said, "Kevin, you are depressed." When he said it like that, I felt stupid again. I had to have known there was something wrong with me. But it was different to give a name to this way I was feeling. I mean, my friends talk about being depressed like having a cold or a headache. It seemed like a much bigger thing when Dr. Mason said it. He made it sound like something real, something people could name and understand. Like maybe he knew that there was some way to deal with this.

Dr. Mason gave me a form to fill out. I had to put a circle around the statements that described how I felt. I almost thought it had been written about me personally. I couldn't concentrate. I couldn't eat. I hated myself. I felt guilty. I felt like I was being punished. I felt so unhappy, I couldn't even cry anymore.

When I gave him back the sheet with all my circles, Dr. Mason and I looked at a book he had, and he showed me the official version of this thing called Major

Depressive Episode. That was me all over again. Somehow, seeing this made me feel better. Like what I was feeling was real, other people had it. Maybe it wasn't all my fault after all. And Dr. Mason told me there was treatment that worked.

He wanted to give me some medicine for the depression. I wasn't sure about this. I didn't want to be doped up with tranquilizers. I wanted to be able to play football (if I ever felt like it again). I imagined my friends thinking I was a psycho-zombie on some kind of pills. But Dr. Mason explained how they work. It seems when you're depressed, you run out of some of your brain chemicals, and the antidepressant medicines help those chemicals come back to normal. Somehow that fit exactly with how I was feeling, like I'd run out of steam. Medicine didn't seem like such a bad idea.

We talked about how the drugs work. It was a bit disappointing at first. They work slowly. Very slowly, I found out. It takes weeks. And meantime, I felt a little weird for a few days. My stomach was a bit upset. I had a headache, but I'm not sure that was due to the drug, because I got them a lot anyway. I felt jumpy or jittery like I'd had too much coffee. I don't drink coffee much, so that felt very strange. That feeling got better after about two days. And by the end of a week, I was waking up with more energy. I started getting hungrier. I got to school on time. And after a few weeks, I actually began to forget about this depression business, like it was a bad dream that was fading in the morning.

How did my parents feel about all this? That was a whole other story. At first, I didn't even want to tell them. But Dr. Mason said that didn't make sense at all. They needed to know what was happening so they could back me up on things like school. So he called them in with me the next day and explained everything, really professionally, with me in the room listening. It sounded so clear when he explained it all.

Then my parents reacted. My mother started to cry. She went on about how this was all their fault, they had been so selfish, they never should have separated. Then my dad got mad at her, and Dr. Mason had to break up the fight. What a pair of losers, I was thinking. I was embarrassed.

But then the whole story came out. It turned out my mother had been depressed for a long time after my youngest sister was born. I didn't even know it. And my dad thinks depression is just weakness. He hated it when it happened to her. Where does that put *me?* I thought.

Then the rest of it came out. All about my dad's dad, my grandfather, Pete. He died ten years ago in an accident. It turns out he had depression. And, worse, he had this manic-depressive problem, so sometimes he went wild and manic, and other times he got very depressed. Suddenly all the stories I had heard about him made sense. How he could stay in his room for months and not talk to anyone. And then the next year he was the life of the party—so loud and cheerful and outgoing he used to scare me when I was little. My dad gets worried when he sees other people getting depressed because it reminds him of his dad. So he'd try to pretend it wasn't happening.

My head was bursting with all this new information. I couldn't absorb it all, but it seemed so important suddenly. Like there was so much that had been going on that I hadn't understood. Dr. Mason said we had to come back a few times and talk about all of this. When my dad started to protest, Dr. Mason said it was "an order." That's when my mother smiled a bit.

By the time I was over that Major Depressive Episode, it had changed my life in some major ways. My family changed a lot. Sometimes I even feel glad it all happened because a lot of things got sorted out. Between me and my dad especially, and even between my parents.

I changed, too. I found out that some of the things I was doing were making me depressed. Like all that beer. It affects me more than my friends. I didn't believe it at first, but when I tried staying away from it, it made a big difference. I hated to admit that, but I have to be honest with Dr. Mason. He knows too much anyway. I need to keep up my sports all year round, not just in football sea-

son. I seem to need that way of getting my frustrations out, otherwise they build up and get me down.

I guess I was under pressure at school after all. When I talked with my school counselor and got a good course plan set up, I felt better. I guess I was trying to take all those science classes because that's what my dad wanted. I wanted to take more accounting and law courses, and to go to college for a business degree.

And I looked at my friendships more carefully. Some of my so-called friends were just hanging around with me because I had a car and they liked to get to parties easily. Then there were the other ones, who made me feel good in a different way, like they were steady and I could trust them not to put me down or take advantage. Hanging around with the right people makes me feel better, just like breathing healthier air.

I'm not drowning anymore. Sometimes I struggle a bit. Sometimes a lot. But it's easier to come up for air pretty quickly. I do get scared for a minute, and start to panic, as if the depression is closing in on me again. And my parents are still separated. That makes me very sad right now, just to think about it. I guess I hoped, when I got better, they'd just come back together again. I still wonder if that was my fault, but Dr. Mason teases me and says I shouldn't think I'm so important as all that. Actually, it's a relief to think that I'm not responsible for everything.

Stacey's Diary

November 10

My mother is a witch! She reads my mind. She reads my diary. She raids my room. And now she's threatening

to lock me in the loony bin. She says I'm the one whose crazy. She's making me that way! She keeps telling me she's worried about me. She thinks I'm "depressed." No wonder. So why doesn't she leave me alone so I can be happy?

My life used to be happier. Now I'm so stressed I can't stand it. I want to eat all the time. Chocolate. Bread.

Chips. Anything. I'm not hungry—I'm empty. And no matter what I eat, it's the same. Empty. I cry a lot. I stayed in my room all weekend. Looking at old pictures. Curled up with my cat. She's the only one I want to be with. She doesn't criticize me. I sleep and I wake up. The days get mixed up. It doesn't matter to me because they're all the same—awful. I keep my blinds pulled down and my light off. I hate looking at myself, so I covered the mirror with a poster.

She stands at my door screaming at me to come out and eat. I cover my head with a pillow and turn up the music. Then an hour later she shouts at me to pass out the dirty plates because the cockroaches are coming. I open the door a crack and pass them through. I'm not sure why I bother. Cockroaches won't even come near this place, it's so depressing.

None of this would be happening if she'd just leave me alone.

December 12

The most gruesome thing happened today. I can't believe she had the nerve. A shrink made a house call. Imagine that! My mother is a witch. She can get anything done she wants.

She talked to our family doctor last week and told her this bunch of lies about what was happening to me. Like it all started when I broke up with my boyfriend. Like I wouldn't go to school because his friends were bugging me. Like my best girlfriend was going out with him now. That I was upset because my dad never writes or calls me. Who cares!

Well, the doctor bought the whole script, and called me on the phone. When I wouldn't talk to her, she came to the house. I was so embarrassed when she knocked on my door. I was going to pretend I wasn't there, but that seemed pretty stupid. So I came out and mumbled some polite stuff to her about everything was okay really. I was just tired and a bit sick and I'd go to school tomorrow. Really. Then I shot daggers at my mother with my eyes. She pretended to be so innocent. I went back to my room.

Then, today, the shrink came. My mother is a witch, I tell you.

The psychiatrist was a reincarnation of Freud. Honestly. Complete with beard and little round glasses. Only a younger version. This time I wouldn't come out of my room. I wasn't falling for that trick again. But after having him wait at the door for about fifteen minutes, I felt so stupid that I did give in. I let him in. That meant my mother came, too. What a scene. The three of us sitting in the dark in the midst of all the mess. I noticed it did smell kind of bad with all the old dishes on the floor.

We had to talk about it all. It was like the whole script was written, and I had to play my part. Yes, my boyfriend dumped me. Yes, my girlfriend had turned on me. Yes, I hated how I looked. Yes, I spent hours trying to fix myself up. Yes, my diet is terrible. Yes, I never get any exercise. Yes, school was hard. Yes, I wished my dad would care to call even once every few months, even if it is long distance. Yes, I hated my mother.

I glanced around at that, watching to see if I got to her. It was a shock to see her face. She was crying. I got confused. Witches don't cry. Then I started to cry, too. And the whole picture kind of dissolved.

My room looked small and gray and lonely instead of safe and warm. It was like I was a prisoner in my anger

and hate and sadness. I felt like I'd served my time, and I wanted to burst out of this jail.

It was a very weird day.

January 15

My psychiatrist told me I was the one who had to let myself out of prison. He said I was the one who had accused myself. I was the judge and jury. I was the one who had sentenced myself to this punishment. And I was the only one who could let me out.

I didn't like that idea. I felt so sure my mother had been the one to set it all up. Maybe she was just a good witness, conveniently ready with evidence that I was a criminal. "No wonder your dad doesn't call if you treat him like that." "You're so self-centered, no wonder your boyfriend couldn't stand you anymore." She has apologized, I guess, but I still think sometimes that's what she believes.

My psychiatrist says it wasn't my fault. That I didn't have much of a chance. So many things have happened to me since I was little. So many hurts. So many disappointments. And every time I tried to figure things out or help myself, my mother would criticize me because I had it wrong somehow. How could I ever learn that things could get better, or that there was anything I could do to make a difference? But he thinks I'm pretty smart, so I can still learn. He's a bit of a stiff, but I am getting to like him more. And I'm starting to believe him, too.

January 28

I don't really mind talking to the shrink anymore. I guess it's helping a bit. What I can't believe is that he's giving me homework, and I'm doing it! As long as no one else finds out. He's been telling me that my negative thinking is making me miserable. I thought it was the other way around. Maybe it's a vicious circle.

Most of my homework is pretty boring. I try not to let my mother know about it, because she'd say, " I told you

so." I'm supposed to get outside more, eat regularly, go to bed and get up at sensible times. I hate the fact that this works, but it does make my energy better. And somehow it's harder to hold onto that miserable prisoner mood if I'm out for a walk in the sunshine.

Some of my homework is very specific. I have to practice looking at people when they talk to me, saying "Hi" first in the hall at school, making phone calls, and making plans for the weekend. I have to practice putting my worries into a mental "treasure box," and only taking

them out during a "worry time" I've decided on. That's to give me control over my talent for imagining the worst. I have to practice thinking up all the ways things could go right, not just the ways things could go wrong. Then I have to keep track of my successes in a little notebook. I feel like some geeky scientist. But I have to admit it does feel good to go back to my psychiatrist and let him know how well I've done.

Some of the homework is hard. I had to write a letter to my dad about how I feel. I don't have to send it, but even writing it is hard. I'm still working on that one.

Another hard thing is the meetings with my mother. I get so mad at her, I feel like screaming. My shrink says that if we can't figure out how to talk about basic things like chores and schedules on our own, we have to do it with him. I guess I'd rather do it on our own, because I feel stupid not to be able to even talk to her. So I'm working on that, too. I guess she is working on it a bit, too, but she still always thinks she's right. I've figured out that she's a perfectionist. Maybe that's where I get it from.

April 6

I hardly ever write in my diary anymore. Just a few notes about where I've been and what I'm doing. I'm spending more time on my drawing. And I'm helping with sets for the school play. I still storm around the house and yell at my mother when I'm feeling stressed. And I haven't sent that letter to my dad yet.

But I'm feeling like my probation is over and I'm back in the world. I forgave my girlfriend, but I still know she was mean, kicking me when I was down. I feel scared somedays, especially before my period, when I start to feel closed in and depressed for a day or two. But the door is wide open, and I can walk out of that prison whenever I want. It's up to me. And I like that feeling of freedom.

RESOURCES

◆

People

You don't need to feel alone. Besides family members, you can turn to school counselors, your doctor, the local mental health center, hospital, or alcohol and drug clinic for information and suggestions for other resources in your area. There probably are support groups or treatment groups available in your area. We know that young people especially benefit from meeting together in a counseling group as part of the treatment for depression.

Books to Help Kids Cope

The Feeling Good Handbook, David Burns. New York: Plume Books, 1989. A practical guide to changing depressive ways of thinking, this book is suggested for older adolescents and adults. It deals with perfectionism, "shoulds," and negative ways of thinking that are part of depression.

Fighting Invisible Tigers: Stress Management for Teens, Earl Hipp. Minneapolis: Free Spirit Publishing, 1985. This practical guide is humorous and effective in teaching skills to recognize and manage stress effectively. Many of these strategies also prevent and help treat depression.

Perfectionism: What's So Bad About Being Too Good? Miriam Adderholdt-Elliott. Minneapolis: Free Spirit Publishing, 1987. Many young people with depression are hard on themselves, imagine the worst in situations, and are generally easily discouraged if they don't do as well as they think they should. This very readable book will help you recognize ways in which "perfectionistic" thinking may be unhelpful, and suggests ways to change this.

Books to Help Parents Understand

Growing Up Sad: Childhood Depression and Its Treatment, Leon Cytryn and Donald H. McKnew, Jr. New York: W.W. Norton, 1996. This is recommended for readers who want to know more about the leading edge of research and the biology of depression.

Helping Your Depressed Teenager: A Guide for Parents and Caregivers, Gerald D. Oster and Sarah S. Montgomery. New York: John Wiley & Sons, 1995. This book is an easy-to-read guide to the assessment and treatment process for depressed and suicidal teenagers, giving plenty of tips on what to look for in good treatment resources.

How to Talk So Kids Will Listen; How to Listen So Kids Will Talk, A. Faber and E. Mazlish. New York: Avon Books, 1980. This is an excellent, classic, and highly recommended book that guides parents on more effective ways of listening and talking to teens to foster good communication. These listening and communicating skills are essential to supporting a depressed young person.

Lonely, Sad and Angry: A Parent's Guide to Depression in Children and Adolescents, Barbara Ingersoll and Sam Goldstein. New York: Doubleday, 1995. A very practical guide to understanding and helping with depression, this book has been highly recommended by parents.

So Young, So Sad, So Listen, Philip Graham and Carol Hughes. London: Gaskell, 1995. Easy-to-read, to-the-point, and humorously illustrated, this book is the most compact guide published for parents. It was prepared by the Royal College of Psychiatrists in Britain and the West London Health Promotion Agency, and is recommended to parents, teachers, siblings, and even depressed teens themselves.

Support Groups

There are local chapters and local support groups in all regions. Contact the main offices listed below for suggestions, or speak with your local mental health clinic or hospital for contact numbers. The Internet World Wide Web also has many helpful ideas and on-line support. These resources change often, so the best approach is to search under "Depression" and you will get an up-to-date list.

National Depressive and Manic-Depressive Association, 730 North Franklin Street, Suite 501, Chicago, IL 60610. Phone: 800-82NDMDA, 312-642-0049; fax: 312-642-7243. Offers support, referrals by telephone, contacts for local chapters

National Mental Health Association, 1021 Prince Street, Alexandria VA 22314-2971.

Canadian Mental Health Association, 2160 Yonge Street, 3rd Floor, Toronto, Ont. M4S 2Z3; 416-484-7750.

A MESSAGE TO PARENTS

◆

This book is written to help young people understand and recover from symptoms of depression. By reading it yourself, you will also have many of your own questions answered. However, you may have other concerns about how you can help. It is hard to watch your child, of any age, struggling, suffering and not getting anywhere. Often, however, your depressed child doesn't seem to want your help or is too irritable to accept your efforts to help. Parents become frustrated and discouraged as well.

Here are some ideas to help you out.

1. Help with actions, not just words.

- ◆ Instead of nagging your teen to get out and exercise, encourage them gently and join them for a walk or a swim. It's a chance to be together, to help them out, and it might be even good for you, too.
- ◆ Organize the household so that daily routines for meals and activities are maintained.
- ◆ Encourage effort rather than results. Praise and support small steps. Depressed adolescents may not maintain previous grades, but if they go to school regularly and do all their homework, that is a good effort, and it will pay off when their mood and concentration improve.

2. Avoid both guilt and blame.

◆ Don't waste your precious energy on guilt, agonizing, or arguing over "the cause" of depression. This energy will be needed for more productive action. As this book describes, the causes of depression are very complex. It is not helpful to blame yourself, your child, your spouse, or your teenager's friends. However, there *are* things you can do right now that will help make things better.

3. Advocate for your child at school and with health professionals involved in their care.

◆ *Advocate at school.* Depressed teenagers don't have the energy or confidence to ask for the support and services they need: tutoring, study periods, and extra opportunities to make up missed work. Sometimes, school staff may not understand depression, seeing the problem as "a bad attitude." As a parent, you can let them know that this is not how you see it. You may need to obtain letters from the doctor to spell out your son's or daughter's entitlement to special academic consideration for medical reasons.

◆ *Advocate for resources.* Find out what kinds of educational supports, counseling, teen groups, and other resources your school and community have available. You know your child's history and temperament well, so you can recognize the kind of setting that may suit them best.

◆ *Advocate for health care.* Confidentiality is very

important for young people dealing with depression. However, you need to have information and advice in order to be sure that you are being effective in your efforts to help. Meeting with the doctor, psychiatrist, or counselor with your child is a good idea. Often it is helpful for the whole family to meet together to make sure everyone's questions are answered. You need to have this contact to feel confident in the care your child is receiving.

4. Be a cheerleader.

Be patient and celebrate small gains. Keep in mind the time course of depression because your child will lose sight of it. Recovery is slow but steady. Psychological treatments and medications take a month or more to work. Things will get better.

Because recovery from depression takes time, it is hard to keep perspective. Young people often begin to feel that "nothing is working." You can help by pointing out small improvements, good efforts, and anticipated continued improvement. If you sense a lot of discouragement, let the doctor or counselors know that this is happening, so that they can address this, too. While the physical symptoms of depression may improve quite quickly, confidence and thinking patterns take longer.

5. Support change in the rest of the family.

A crisis like depression is an opportunity to look at the whole family's lifestyle and coping strategies. The healthier people in the family can model and support change in the depressed person. Many families decide that some kind of family counseling would be helpful to deal with this crisis or to address other issues that may have contributed to it. Siblings may need a chance to talk about their feelings. Often they think the depressed person is getting some unfair advantages or extra attention because of their illness. They may need to talk with the doctor as well to understand what is happening.

Depression in a child sometimes signals an unresolved family problem such as marital conflict, and this must be addressed for the depression to get better. In most cases, families need to look at their communication style. Busy, stressed families often fall into a pattern of critical, frustrated interactions. Families are encouraged to start using negotiation, contracting, verbal encouragement, and positive reinforcement instead of fruitless arguing, which leaves everyone feeling bad. Sometimes one of the parents is depressed at the same time as the child, and this needs to be addressed for everyone's sake.

For many families, a crisis like depression in a young person leads them to make positive changes and eventually understand each other better.

6. Seek support for yourself.

A parent needs to be clear-thinking and strong to support a child at this time. Consider a parent support group, individual counselor, or your own personal support network through your extended family, church, or community. Lean on those people who offer constructive support, not blame.

Look at your own stress management strategies. Perhaps you could benefit from some of the changes in sleep patterns, exercise, and time management suggested in this book.

7. Gradually increase expectations with recovery.

When adolescents are ill, expectations are removed. They may not have to do chores and they may be given special allowance compared to other family members. However, as they improve, you can show your confidence in them by slowly restoring expectations for responsibilities around the house. This phase can be quite challenging, and you may want to talk with a counselor or health professional involved in the treatment of your child to get some guidance on how quickly to shift things toward normal.

8. Get more information.

Ask lots of questions of your doctor, psychiatrist, psychologist, or other professionals involved. You may be directed to a support group for families of depressed individuals, as listed in the Resources section. In addition, this section lists several books written especifically for parents. These are recommended if you want more in-depth understanding of depression and how you can help.